AF437851

Luqman's Fifty Pearls of Wisdom

Shaykh Abdur Razzaaq al Badr

Contents

Introduction

Indeed all praise is due to Allaah. We praise Him, seek His forgiveness and ask Him for help. We seek refuge with Allaah from the evil of ourselves and the evils of our actions. Whoever Allaah guides, then no one can lead him astray. Whoever Allaah misguides then there is no guidance for him. I testify that there is nothing worthy of worship except Allaah, and I testify that Muhammad is his slave and his messenger – Peace and Blessings of Allaah be upon him, his family, and all his companions.

To proceed:

Indeed the well-known advice in the story of Luqmaan has many great benefits, wisdoms, noble guidance, blessed gestures, correct approaches to calling to Allaah, and raising children and upbringing generations. In it is a way to success and effective methods in calling to Allaah – Most High – and educating the people about the good. Due to this, the educators, fathers, and teachers must certainly pay attention to this advice and contemplate at these points to take from it the effective approach and the guided way in *dawah* (calling towards Allaah) and teaching, in addition to what is in this advice from the methods of the wise one (Luqmaan) to fetch the hearts and to pull the minds, and to awaken interest and to warn, and good advice, and a good entrance upon the people in clarifying the good to them, and calling them to the religion of Allaah – the Most High.

Dawah is the knowledge that is called to and action that it guides towards. For it requires wisdom, beneficial means, and influential methods until it enters the hearts of the people. Allaah – the Most High – gave His servant Luqmaan the Wisdom and preserved this wisdom in his heart. And He made Luqmaan's speech, counsel, education, and guidance as wisdom.

All of this is an example for us to contemplate, think, and to study this advice that Allaah – the Most High – noted in His Book, the Noble Quraan.

Allaah said (in the Noble Quran):

*12) And indeed We bestowed upon Luqmaan Al-Hikmah (wisdom and religious understanding, etc.)
saying: "Give thanks to Allaah,"
and whoever gives thanks, he gives thanks for (the good of) his own self.
And whoever is unthankful, then verily,
Allaah is All Rich (Free of all wants), Worthy of all praise.*

*13) And (remember) when Luqmaan said to his son when he was advising him:
"O my son! Join not in worship others with Allaah.
Verily! Joining others in worship with Allaah is a great Zulm (wrong or oppression) indeed.*

14) And We have enjoined on man (to be dutiful and good) to his parents.

*His mother bore him in weakness and hardship upon
weakness and hardship,
and his weaning is in two years –
give thanks to Me and to your parents,
unto Me is the final destination.*

*15) But if they (both) strive with you to make you
join in worship with Me others that of which you
have no knowledge,
then obey them not,
but behave with them in the world kindly,
and follow the path of him who turns to Me in
repentance and in obedience.
Then to Me will be your return,
and I shall tell you what you used to do.*

*16) "O my son! If it be (anything) equal to the weight
of a grain of mustard seed,
and though it be in a rock,
or in the heavens or in the earth,
Allaah will bring it forth.
Verily, Allaah is Subtle (in bringing out that grain),
Well Aware (of its place).*

*17) "O my son! Perform The Prayer,
enjoin (people) for Al-Ma'ruf (Islaamic Monotheism
and all that is good),
and forbid (people) from Al-Munkar (that is disbelief
in the Oneness of Allaah, polytheism of all kinds and
all that is evil and bad),
and bear with patience whatever befall you.*

Verily! These are some of the important commandments ordered by Allaah with no exemption.

*18) And turn not your face away from men with pride,
nor walk in insolence through the earth.
Verily, Allaah likes not each arrogant boaster.*

*19) And be moderate (or show no insolence) in your walking,
and lower your voice.
Verily, the most detestable of all voices is the voice (braying) of the donkey.*

Speaking about this (advice) in this noble context will be a narrative of benefits that are derived from these noble verses. I have counted – briefly – (about) fifty benefits. I ask Allaah to benefit us with it and grant us a good benefit from this blessed wise advice (of Luqmaan).

Note: Luqmaan is a righteous servant of Allaah and not a Prophet. There is no evidence in the Quraan or the Sunnah of the Prophet – Peace and Blessings of Allaah be upon him – that proves that he is a prophet. Imaam al-Baghawee – Allaah have Mercy upon him – said in his Tafseer (explanation of the Quraan) that there is agreement regarding that. He said, "The scholars have agreed that he was a wise person and not a prophet, except Ikrimah for he said, 'Luqmaan was a Prophet', and he was alone in that statement." (Ma'aalim at-Tanzeel (3/490)

"And indeed We bestowed upon Luqmaan Al-Hikmah (wisdom and religious understanding, etc.) ..."

Soorah Luqmaan

Wisdom 1

Wisdom is a privilege and a gift from Allaah. He gives it to whom He wishes from His slaves. This is based on His statement:

And indeed We bestowed upon Luqmaan Al-Hikmah (wisdom and religious understanding, etc.)

So wisdom is (from) the mercy of Allaah that He bestows upon who He wills from His slaves, as He said:

He grants Hikmah (wisdom) to whom He pleases, and he, to whom Hikmah is granted, is indeed granted abundant good. But none remember (will receive admonition) except men of understanding.

And whoever wants to be granted this (wisdom), and every good, then he must seek it from Allaah (alone), because all good and bounties are in the hand of Allaah (the Most High). He gives it to whom He wants and Allaah is owner of great bounties.

Good is not attained except by being honest with Allaah, turning to Him (alone), being obedient to Him and seeking *tawfeeq* (being granted the ability to act) from Him, and seeking help in attaining that from Him, because truly guidance and *tawfeeq* is in His hands, and He has no partners.

Wisdom 2

Wisdom must be (gained) through ways the slave (that is the one obedient to Allaah) takes, and whoever ponders the story of Luqmaan the Wise and looks also into his life (story) will find that he was a good righteous slave and worshiper of Allaah (the Most High), turning to His obedience, and he made the best of his relationship with his Lord. And it is reported in his biography, as mentioned by Al-Haafidh Ibn Katheer (Allaah have mercy on him) and other than him from the people of knowledge, that he (that is Luqmaan) was a person of worship and turning to Allaah (the Most High) and honesty, and he spoke little and thought and contemplated much, and he used to benefit from the sittings of good, and he encouraged others to benefit from them, and (encouraged others to take) advice from the people of knowledge and benefit from them. The point being that the slave gains goodness and success by exerting all useful means (and doing actions) that bring a person close to Allaah (the Most High), and with it he also gains wisdom. Due to this the Prophet (peace and blessings of Allaah be upon him) said:

Work hard (or strive) for that which will benefit you, and seek the help of Allaah.

He (peace and blessings of Allaah be upon him) also said:

Truly knowledge is from learning, and *hilm* (forbearance and insight - wisdom) is by developing *hilm*, and whoever seeks good is given it, and whoever avoids evil is protected from it.

Therefore it is absolutely necessary that we exert all means that lead to (gaining of) wisdom, and it is not sufficient for the slave to (only) say: "O Allaah, give me wisdom", or "O Allaah, verily I ask you for beneficial knowledge and righteous deeds", without exerting efforts (doing actions) in reaching those means (of acquiring wisdom).

Allaah (the Most High) says:

So worship Him and put your trust in Him.

And He (Allaah) says:

You (Alone) we worship, and you (Alone) we ask for help (for each and everything).

Wisdom 3

The importance of thanking for the favors of Allaah and the greatness of the effect it has on the endurance, preservation, growth, and increase of the favor (or blessing).

Allaah said:

And indeed We bestowed upon Luqmaan Al-Hikmah (wisdom and religious understanding) saying: "Give thanks to Allaah"

And the blessing remains if one is grateful (to Allaah for it), and departs if one is ungrateful. Due to this, some of the scholars call *shukr* (thankfulness) al-haafidh (or that which preserves) or al-jaalib (or that which brings), because it keeps the blessings that are present and brings the blessings that are not, as Allaah (the Most High) said:

And (remember) when your Lord proclaimed: "If you give thanks (by accepting Faith and worshipping none but Allaah), I will give you more (of My Blessings) ..."

and as Allaah said:

Give thanks to Allaah

Meaning to give thanks to Allaah for the blessings bestowed upon you and His favors and generosity. And from His generosity, Glory be to Him, to this righteous slave (Luqmaan) is that He gave him wisdom and granted him success with beneficial knowledge and good deeds, and in this is a clear indication that if the slave is granted success to have knowledge and action and good, then it is upon him to be forever grateful to Allaah (the Most High) recognizing the favor of Allaah upon him and His bounty and guidance and *tawfeeq*.

Wisdom 4

Verily gratefulness for the blessings (and favors) is (done) with the heart, tongue, and limbs. These three are included in the saying of Allaah:

Give thanks to Allaah.

And whoever is given wisdom and beneficial knowledge and righteous deeds, then gratitude for that is in his heart by recognizing the blessings of the *Mun'im* (the One who bestowed) and it is with the tongue by praising Allaah and thanking, and with the limbs by using the blessings in obedience to Allaah (the Most High) as Allaah said:

"Work you, O family of Dawud (David), with thanks!"...

So the slave (of Allaah) performs righteous actions and is diligent in obedient actions, and in using the blessings in the way and path that Allaah (the Most High) ordered it to be used in.

Wisdom 5

That verily Allaah does not benefit from the appreciation of those who thank or the ingratitude of the ungrateful, as he said:

"Give thanks to Allaah," and whoever gives thanks, he gives thanks for (the good of) his own self. And whoever is unthankful, then verily, Allaah is All-Rich (Free of all wants), Worthy of all praise...

So Allaah does not benefit from the gratefulness of the person who thanks and is not harmed by the ungratefulness of the person who is ungrateful, and He does not benefit from the obedience of the person who obeys and is not harmed by the disobedience of the person who disobeys; so think about this in regards to the statement of Allaah (the Most High) in the Hadeeth Qudsi related by Abu Dharr (Allaah be pleased with him) in Saheeh Muslim:

...O my slaves, if the first of you and the last of you, and the human of you and the jinn of you, were all upon the heart of the most pious man amongst you, it would not increase my dominion in anything. O my slaves, if the first of you and the last of you, and the human of you and the jinn of you, were all upon the heart of most wicked man amongst you, it would not decrease from my dominion anything...

Thus He (the Most High) does not benefit from the obedience of the one who obeys, and is not harmed by the disobedience of the one who disobeys, rather the person who goes right, then he goes right only for the benefit of his own self. And the person who goes astray, then he goes astray to his own loss.

> *O mankind! it is you who stand in need of Allaah,
> but Allaah is Rich (Free of all wants and needs),
> Worthy of all praise. If He wills, He could destroy
> you and bring about a new creation.*

Wisdom 6

Indeed the effect and benefit of the 'abd's (the slave of Allaah) gratitude returns back to himself only.

...and whoever gives thanks, he gives thanks for (the good of) his own self.

So the 'abd, if he gives thanks, his thankfulness returns back to him in both this life and the next. In this life (by keeping) the blessing firm and enduring, and bringing other blessings along with it, as mentioned previously, and in the next life as a reward, requital, and a good recompense. Thus the 'abd if he thanks (Allah for the blessing), his thankfulness returns to him and he benefits from it, and from that is the statement of Allaah (the Most High):

Whoever goes right, then he goes right only for the benefit of his own self. And whoever goes astray, then he goes astray to his own loss.

And if the 'abd, and we seek refuge with Allaah, is ungrateful (to Allah), then his ungratefulness returns upon him as evil (or a curse), grief, and regret in both this life and the next. And at this time it is appropriate for the 'abd to bear in mind that indeed it is he who is in need of being grateful to Allaah, and as for Allaah, then He is not in need of his gratitude.

Wisdom 7

The firm belief that Allaah is totally not in need of anyone in any possible way, and the 'abd totally needs Allaah in every possible way.

And whoever is unthankful, then verily, Allaah is All-Rich (Free of all wants), Worthy of all praise

We believe that Allaah is *ghanee* (that is not in need of anyone or anything), and *Al-Ghanee* is a name from the Most Beautiful Names of Allaah, and it is inclusive of His attribute (the Most High) of being *ghanee*. And He (the Most High) is not in need of His slaves or any of His creation in any way, and all of His slaves and creation are in need of Him in every possible way. And we believe that our Lord (Allaah the Most High) is above His throne, separate from his creation, as He has stated in His book

The Most Beneficent (Allaah) Istawa (rose over) the (Mighty) Throne (in a manner that suits His Majesty).

And

...and then He Istawa (rose over) the Throne (really in a manner that suits His Majesty)

And we believe at the same time that Allaah is not in need of the throne or what is less than it, and that all of the creation, the throne and what is under it, is in need of Allaah. He (the Most High) said:

Verily! Allaah grasps the heavens and the earth lest they move away from their places, and if they were to move away from their places, there is not one that could grasp them after Him. Truly, He is Ever Most Forbearing, Oft-Forgiving.

Therefore He is the One who holds the throne, the sky, the earth, and all of the creation are standing by His will, and they (His creation) are not free from needing Him even for the blink of an eye.

Wisdom 8

Affirmation of the perfection of His praise (the Most High) and that to Him belong all the praise for all of His generous blessings and great names and attributes. He said:

And whoever is unthankful, then verily, Allaah is All-Rich (Free of all wants), Worthy of all praise...

Al-Hameed (meaning Worthy of praise) is a name from the most beautiful names of Allaah, and it indicates the affirmation that all praise are due to Allaah (alone), and that to Him belong the utmost perfect praise in every situation and at every time. Therefore He is praised for His names and attributes, and He is praised for His blessings, and signs, and favors, and gifts. Thus He is *Al-Hameed* and to Him belongs all praise. He said:

His is all praise, in the first (that is in this world) and in the last (that is in the Hereafter).

So to Him is all praise in the beginning and in the end, and to Him is all thanks (or gratitude), in open and in secret. And all praises are due to Allaah (alone), and all blessings are from Allaah, and what the slaves (of Allaah) have in terms of blessings then this is from Allaah and He is their owner, and it is only appropriate that all of the praise be to Allaah alone, the One who bestows. And it is because of this that the people performing pilgrimage say: "Verily all praise and *ni'mah* (blessings) are to You, and the dominion, You have no partners".

Wisdom 9

The status of wisdom and its great benefit to the one that Allaah gives it to, and favors him with attaining it, and this is clear in the context (of this verse) from Allaah's praising Luqmaan because He gave him wisdom, and this makes the '*abd* eager about knowing what wisdom is and eager about being the one having wisdom (being blessed with it). And from what is said about the meaning of wisdom: "It (wisdom) is having beneficial knowledge combined with righteous action", and it is also said: "It is placing affairs in their proper place", and it has also been said: "It is insight, understanding, correctness, and good opinion", and other than that has been said as well.

The point being that wisdom has a great status and it is for the '*abd* to work hard and struggle to attain it by using all permissible means that lead to it (gaining wisdom).

Wisdom 10

The importance of the mannerisms (that are used) when advising (or warning) in raising and educating.

Allaah said:

And (remember) when Luqmaan said to his son when he was advising him...

The mannerisms of advising have a major effect in the nurturing of the people and the education of new generations. Advice (and warning) is as the scholars have said: "That the knowledge which the people are being directed toward and guided toward its implementation is combined with encouragement and discouragement, so that commanding the good is mentioned with things which will encourage that and forbidding the evil or vice is mentioned with that which will discourage that. So advice (and warning) is commanding the good and forbidding the evil with encouragement and discouragement [respectively]. Encouragement takes place by mentioning the benefits and rewards and [good] effects that the ʻabd will attain by doing the actions that he is encouraged to do, and discouragement takes place by mentioning the dangers and harms that are encountered by the person who falls into what is forbidden.

Such is what Luqmaan the Wise did when he included in his advices beautiful encouragement to support the listener to do what he is being called to in the best manner and most perfect condition, as well as preventative discouragement to block the listener from doing sinful and wrong actions.

Wisdom 11

The importance of showing affection (that is by using the manners and words that are pleasing) and its great effect on the one who listens and the one who is learning. When you want to advise or warn a person it is appropriate that you show affection to them (in an appropriate way), by mentioning gentle phrases and beautiful words that will make your speech enter the heart of the listener, and make his heart open up to your speech. Notice that Luqmaan used beautiful words when talking to his son, and effective ways, along with words that enter the heart, and look at his gentleness with his son when advising him, where you find the phrase 'my little son' repeated in the context [of his speech], because this word has a huge effect on the heart of the son, and it has an effect on the soul, and it is an aid in attentiveness, and brings complete benefit, and speech has the greatest effect if it accompanied by affection. If however the advice is far from having affection, for example a person says while he is advising or admonishing, "hey boy" (rude words), or as it is mentioned that when some people address their son or admonish him for something he did, then they call him by the names of some animals; so how will the heart of the one being advised open up to this kind of mannerisms that lead, no doubt, to closing off of one's self and dull the mind.

So what a difference between this way and [the way in which] the advisor uses manners of affection, like the statement of Luqmaan to his son: "O my little son" with compassion, fatherhood [that is speaking like a father would], with emotion, and ease, so that the heart (of his son) opens up. Notice also the affection in the hadeeth of Mu'aadh ibn Jabal (Allaah be pleased with him) than the Prophet (peace and blessings of Allaah be upon him) took him by the hand one day and then said "O Mu'aadh! Verily I love you" So Mu'aadh replied, "bi abi anta waummi [that is I would give my father and mother for you] O Messenger of Allaah, and I love you too." He said: "I advise you O Mu'aadh, after every salaah, do not ever leave off saying (the prayer), 'O Allaah, help me upon Your remembrance, and Your thanks, and the best of worship to You."

So [in the hadeeth] he (peace and blessings of Allaah be upon him) began with affection and ease so that he [that is Mu'adh – Allaah be pleased with him] would be receptive to the benefit (from the speech), and the secrets of the heart would open, and he would become prepared for receiving (the advice). So this is what must be done when calling to Allaah (the Most High) and when teaching the people good.

Wisdom 12

Paying attention to the priorities in calling to Allaah. Parents, educators, and callers to Allaah (the Most High) should pay attention to this when calling the people to good, and should begin with the most important (issue) and then speak about the least important. Even in raising children and upbringing generations we begin first with instilling the correct belief (the *aqeedah* according to the salaf – the companions and the first three generations) and beneficial *imaan* (faith), then after this they are taught worship and etiquette and manners. Based on this when the Prophet (peace and blessings of Allaah be upon him) sent Mu'aadh ibn Jabal (Allaah be pleased with him) to Yemen, he said to him: "Verily you are going to a people from the people of the Book, so let the first thing you call them to be that they single out Allaah ta'aalaa" [that is singling out Allaah in worship, meaning that they worship Allaah alone and not ascribe partners to Him].

And this is how Luqmaan the Wise advised when he wanted to advise his son with a number of beneficial advices that he needed to be advised with; He began with saying:

O my son! Join not in worship others with Allaah.

Wisdom 13

That *shirk* (associating partners with Allaah, whether in belief or in action - that is worshiping other than Allaah in any form at all regardless of the reasoning) is the greatest and most dangerous of all sins, and it is the greatest of what Allaah has prohibited. This is understood from Luqmaan the Wise beginning (his advice) with it while warning from the most dangerous of all affairs. This is the way of those who sincerely advise when they forbid from dangerous matters, they begin with the worst of them and the most dangerous of them, and as such Luqmaan the Wise [began] with by prohibiting his son from *shirk*.

And it should be noted from this blessed context that he (Luqmaan) forbids him (his son) from a number of different issues: he prohibited him from arrogance, delusion, and showing off, but the first thing he began with was prohibiting shirk with Allaah. So this (the order of Luqmaan's advice) shows that shirk is the most dangerous of affairs and the most harmful of them.

Wisdom 14

The importance of bringing up the children from a young age upon *tawheed* [true monotheism that is that they worship nothing besides Allaah] and upon sincerity, and being distant from *shirk*, and this is also understood from this advice.

O my son! Join not in worship others with Allaah.

So, the children need to be warned from *shirk* and called to *tawheed* and sincerity from a small age. So if the child is instilled with *tawheed* from the beginning of his youth it will benefit him with a great benefit, with the permission of Allaah.

Because of this it is also from wisdom to name the children - Abdullah and Abdur-Rahmaan [that is meaning the servant of Allaah and the servant of the Most Beneficent, respectively], as it comes in the hadeeth: "The best of names are Abdullah and Abdur-Rahmaan". With these names the child may grow up upon *tawheed* (worshipping and asking help from Allaah alone) and knowing that he is a servant of [and should always obey] Allaah and not his desires, or the worldly life, or satan, or the fortune of his self, but rather be a servant of Allaah (the Most High). So, he grows up upon the principals of *imaan* (faith), and the foundations of the sound belief (aqeedah), and it is the foundation for which the *deen* [religion and life style] is built, and the *millah* [creed or religion] is founded upon it, and it is the foundation that the religion stands upon. So, the religion will not stand and the millah will not be upright except upon *tawheed* and sincerity to Allaah (the Most High).

Wisdom 15

Shirk is the worst (that is the most oppressive) form of oppression, and it is the biggest crime, and this is understood from the statement:

Verily! Joining others in worship with Allaah is a great Zulm (wrong) indeed.

And *zulm* (oppression) is placing something in other than its appropriate place, and which *zulm* is worse than placing worship in other than its place, such that it is given to creation who lacks and is incompetent [or unable to do what is needed], does not possess for himself any benefit or harm, or life or resurrection, so which sin is worse than this (*shirk*)?

Allaah created the human and then he (the human) turns to worship to someone other than Him (that is his Creator Allaah). Allaah provides for him and he turns to ask for provision from other than Him, and Allaah cures him and he turns and seeks to be cured from other than Him, so which *zulm* is worse than this (*shirk*)?

Wisdom 16

The need of the learner and the one being called, to know the fruits of [obeying] the commands and the dangers of [falling into] the forbidden, so that he may be able to implement that [that is perform the commands and avoid the forbidden]. So if the command is mentioned to him then (we should also mention) a benefit and fruit [of its action]. And if a prohibition is mentioned to him then the punishment and consequences that come to the one who does the forbidden action need to mentioned as well, and this wisdom is taken from a number of places in the advice of Luqmaan.

Wisdom 17

This advice also contains the wisdom to be dutiful to parents, good to them, generous to them, and minding the rights of the parents, and this is [found] in His statement.

And We have enjoined on man (to be dutiful and good) to his parents.
His mother bore him in weakness and hardship upon weakness and hardship,
and his weaning is in two years give thanks to Me and to your parents,
unto Me is the final destination.

Therefore advising with [obedience to the] parents has great significance, and this advice pertains to great affairs [that is affairs of great importance], and the advice here is from the Lord of the Worlds (the Most High). Due to this more than one of the *mufassireen* (the scholars who explained the Quraan) said that verily His statement:

And We have enjoined on man (to be dutiful and good) to his parents,

came interrupting the advice of Luqmaan that Allaah mentioned, as advise from Him (the Most High) with being good to parents.

So then from the great wisdoms of this blessed advice is the advice of being dutiful to parents, knowing their rights, being good to them, being obedient to them, and giving them their rights.

Wisdom 18

From the affairs that help the most in regards to being dutiful to the parents are reminders of the beautiful [actions] of the past, and the good actions that came forth. This helps the person do be dutiful and keeps him away from disobedience and the cutting off ties of the family. Contemplate His statement:

And We have enjoined on man (to be dutiful and good) to his parents. His mother bore him in weakness and hardship upon weakness and hardship, and his weaning is in two years,

meaning, remember O [you] the son what happened to your mother during motherhood, pregnancy, suckling, and raising and education, and think of her pregnancy and her pains and fatigue, and the long time you spent in the womb, a weight that she carries in her belly for nine months and the effort [it takes] to stand and sit and sleep, then the situation becomes more severe and the effort the mother puts at the time of birth until you come out into this life, then the suckling, and what surrounds her from tiredness and pain and sleeplessness; all of these good things should not be forgotten and should not be absent from the mind.

Wisdom 19

From the things which help a person to be obedient (or dutiful) is the remembering that the going and the return is to Allaah. So the one who is obedient to his parents remembers that he will surely return to Allaah and he will meet the reward of his good actions and dutifulness, therefore he increases (because of this) in dutifulness and good deeds, and the one who is bad to his parents remembers that he will surely return to Allaah and meet the punishment of his bad deeds to his parents.

Wisdom 20

The greatness of the rights of the mother and that your mother is the first of people in regards to being dutiful and having good company [that is that she has the priority and first right in these matters]. In the hadeeth, [is it reported] that a man came to the Prophet (peace and blessings of Allaah be upon him) and said, 'O Messenger of Allaah, who has the most rights to my good company?'. The Prophet (peace and blessings of Allaah be upon him) said 'Your mother'. He asked, 'Then who?', the Prophet (peace and blessings of Allaah be upon him) said, 'Then your mother'. He again asked 'Then who?', the Prophet (peace and blessings of Allaah be upon him) said, 'Then your mother'. He asked 'Then who?', the Prophet (peace and blessings of Allaah be upon him) said, 'Then your father'.

So he mentioned the mother three times because she has more right and she is first in regards to your good companionship, and also because the good that the son [or child] received from the mother is not like, or even close to what he received from someone other than her. Because of this some of the scholars said that truly in this verse is a proof and support for the statement of the Prophet (peace and blessings of Allaah be upon him) 'Your mother, then your mother, then your mother', and that is such because Allaah (the Most High) mentioned in this context the mother three stages of her goodness to the son:

The first is motherhood,

The second is pregnancy,

The third is breastfeeding and his weaning.

[from the verse mentioned above:

And We have enjoined on man (to be dutiful and good) to his parents. His mother bore him in weakness and hardship upon weakness and hardship, and his weaning is in two years.]

So these three stages [or levels of good] from the mother did not happen because of the father or anyone else at all who may have done good deeds to the son [or child]. And this requires that the beautiful [actions] and good be returned with good, and this also requires that she be the person who has the most rights to your good companionship of all the people. However from the greatest trials is that you find some people who received from their mother long lasting good deeds and continuous beautiful actions, then in the end they give their dutifulness and kindness and good companionship to others who never gave him a tenth of a tenth [or a tenth of a fraction] of what his mother put forth, and he doesn't give his mother anything from good companionship, and even if he gives her, he gives her what little is left over. Is this how a person returns the beautiful and good actions and how he rewards the good doers!? And for this reason being bad to a person's mother is one of the worst (major) sins and one of the most blameworthy action. How can a person treat his mother badly when she is the best of those who put forth good towards him, treated him well, and was generous to him?

Wisdom 21

What the mother went through during the pregnancy and delivery in regards to difficulty and pain is something that the son will never able to reach in its recompense [that is he will never be able to repay his mother for it] no matter how much he strives to be dutiful and hard working (towards her).

Wisdom 22

Placing the rights of the parents next to the rights of Allaah [in the verse] shows the greatness of the status of their rights [that is the parents], and that it is from the most obligatory of rights after the rights of Allaah. And in many places in the Quraan where Allaah places His rights next to the rights of the parents.

Wisdom 23

Thanking the parents is [done] by loving them, praying for them, being righteous towards them, keeping ties with them, and being good to them.

Wisdom 24

The danger of being bad (evil behavior) to the parents and that it is from the worst of sins and this is from the most blameworthy of deeds.

And [it is narrated] in the Sahihain [that is Saheeh Al-Bukhaari and Saheeh Muslim] from the hadeeth of Abi Bakrah (Allaah be pleased with him) [that] he said, the Messenger of Allaah (peace and blessings of Allaah be upon him) said, "Should I not inform you of the worst of the worst sins", three times. They said, 'Of course O Messenger of Allaah'. He said, "Al-ishraak billah [associating partners with Allaah], being disobedient to the parents", then he sat up, and he was reclining, then he said, "and surely the false statement." He did not stop repeating it until we said if only he would stop.

[It is important to note that the Companions (Allaah be pleased with him) were not being rude by thinking this, although it may appear that way when translated, but rather they said this because they did not want to see the Prophet (peace and blessings of Allaah be upon him) upset, as Imaam An-Nawawi explains in his explanation of Muslim]

Wisdom 25

The way to interact with a father and mother if they are polytheists or open sinners, as Allaah says:

But if they (both) strive with you to make you join in worship with Me others that of which you have no knowledge, then obey them not, but behave with them in the world kindly...

Both the father and mother are not obeyed if they request from their child that he associate partners with Allaah or that he do a sin. However, at the same time he must be in good companionship (have good manners) with them.

Wisdom 26

The completeness of the Shari'ah (that is the Islaamic laws and rulings) in its call to preserve the good, and its taking care of that which is beautiful, and this becomes clear when the father or mother being polytheists call their child to *shirk* (that is ascribing partners with Allaah), because Allaah [says]:

Behave with them in the world kindly.

This (the command to behave with them in a good manner) is if they are polytheists, so what about [or how much more should the good behavior of the child be] if they are believers and when they order only that which is good, and not calling except to righteousness and kindness.

Wisdom 27

There is no obedience to the creation if it involves disobedience to the Creator. Allaah says:

But if they (the parents) strive with you to make you join in worship with Me others that of which you have no knowledge, then obey them not, but behave with them in the world kindly...

Wisdom 28

There can be from the people of misguidance and falsehood those who fight, exert all efforts, and spend all their energy for spreading their falsehood and calling to their misguidance, and this is clear in the statement:

But if they (your parents) strive with you

Wisdom 29

Differentiating [or separating or making a distinction] between not obeying and being *'uqooq* [which is blameworthy disobedience]. But some people join these affairs and make them the same, but what is correct is that there is a difference between them.

Allaah said:

then obey them not

but did not say "so be disobedient to them" [that is with blameworthy disobedience].

Wisdom 30

The virtue of the companions of the Prophet (peace and blessings of Allah be upon him) and they being the best of the Ummah (the nation of all Muslims from the time of the Prophet). This is taken from His statement:

and follow the path of him who turns to Me in repentance and in obedience.

And if you look at the condition of the companions, and the best people of the Ummah, you will find that their condition is a condition of those who turn to Allaah (the Most High) in repentance and obedience. And for this reason, you find some of the mufassireen (scholars who explained the Quraan) saying [in regards to the verse]

and follow the path of him who turns to Me in repentance and in obedience.

This refers to Abu Bakr, and some say

and follow the path of him who turns to Me in repentance and in obedience.

means the companions.

This is all explanation of the text with part of its pieces or with the best of them [that is parts of the whole, being the companions from all of the people who fit this category, or the best companion, meaning Abu

Bakr (Allaah be pleased with him) from all those who fit this category]. And this shows us the virtue of the Sahaabah and the virtue of the best of the Ummah, and that we should know the path of these great examples, and follow their path, and warn against following other than the path of the Believers.

And whoever contradicts and opposes the Messenger (Muhammad peace and blessings of Allaah be upon him) after the right path has been shown clearly to him, and follows other than the believers' way. We shall keep him in the path he has chosen, and burn him in Hell - what an evil destination.

Wisdom 31

The importance of choosing your friends (or companions), since it is not for the believer to sit with anyone he wishes [that is be in their company]. And how many bad things may possibly occur to a person because of [his] friend (or companion). So the *'abd* (the servant of Allaah) is ordered not to sit with everyone, but rather to sit with (or be in the company of) the people of good, virtue, and excellence. And this is taken from His statement

and follow the path of him who turns to Me in repentance and in obedience.

Wisdom 32

Al-Inaabah (turning back to Allaah in repentance and obedience) includes four things: Love for Him, being submissive to Him, turning to Him, and rejecting other than Him.

Ibn Al-Qayyim (Allaah have mercy on him) said: "So the name *Al-Muneeb* (the one who turns in repentance and obedience) is not deserving of anyone except the person who has brought together these four things in himself, and the explanation of the Salaf for this word revolves around that".

Wisdom 33

The actions of the servants of Allaah are all gathered [and accounted for and] they will find it present on the Day of Judgement.

Then to Me will be your return, and I shall tell you what you used to do

Wisdom 34

There is no clear evidence for [the validity of] *shirk* or proof for its people [that is that the people of *shirk* have no evidence for their actions]. This is taken from His statement.

But if they (both) strive with you to make you join in worship with Me others that of which you have no knowledge

And this is similar to His statement:

And whoever invokes (or worships), besides Allaah, any other ilah (god), of whom he has no proof

So shirk, in whatever form it may be or whatever meaning it may have, has no proof [for its validity]. This is a fixed attribute of shirk in all its conditions and all its forms.

Wisdom 35

The importance of firmly establishing [that is reassuring and reminding of] a person's return to Allaah and the recompensing of the *'abd* (the servant of Allaah) for what he has put forth in this life, when calling the people to good and forbidding them from evil. So it is important to have this in mind during *da'wah* (calling to Allaah). And because of the importance of reaffirming this, it was repeated in the story of Luqmaan, in His statement:

...unto Me is the final destination.

And then after it:

Then to Me will be your return

So this is something that people need to be reminded of frequently in order to engrain in their minds their return to Allaah and Allaah's recompensing them for their actions in this life, so that they may do well in preparing and getting ready for the Day of Return.

Wisdom 36

The All-Encompassing Knowledge of Allaah (the Most High) has nothing hidden from Him in the Earth or in the Skies [that is nothing at all]

"O my son! If it be (anything) equal to the weight of a grain of mustard seed, and though it be in a rock, or in the heavens or in the earth, Allaah will bring it forth. Verily, Allaah is Subtle (in bringing out that grain), Well-Aware (of its place)

Wisdom 37

The effect of *Imaan* (belief and action together) in the names and attributes of Allaah in the uprightness of the *'abd* (servant of Allaah) and the purity of his actions, and that the more the *'abd* is knowledgeable about Allaah, the more he will he will be afraid of Him [that is afraid of doing something that displeases Him], and the more he will seek to worship Him, and the farther he will be away from sins. And Luqmaan's reminder of the names and attributes of Allaah were repeated [in the verses- that are mentioned frequently].

Wisdom 38

The importance of raising children with them knowing the supervision of Allaah [that is that Allaah is aware and has full knowledge of everything that we do]. So if you say to your son: "Do not do this", then do not make him watch out for you (that is afraid of you), but rather direct the supervision of Allaah to his actions, so say to him, for example: O my son pray, and stay away from the haraam (that which is forbidden), because Allaah sees you, and watches you, and nothing from you escapes Him (or his hidden to Him), and if you were to make so a small wrong deed, and if this was wrong was done in a blocked off stony place, or in the sky, or in the depths of the earth, Allaah will bring it on the Day of Resurrection, so be careful my son (be afraid of Allaah)! So be mindful of Allaah (the Most High). And how mighty is the benefit of this education to the children.

Wisdom 39

On the Day of Resurrection the scales will be [measured] in the weight of *adh-dharrah* (a small ant or a small particle).

Therefore, whoever does good equal to the weight of an atom (or a small ant), then he shall see it (his good action). And whoever does an evil equal to the weight of an atom (or a small ant), then he shall see it.

And this is taken from His statement:

"... If it be (anything) equal to the weight of a grain of mustard seed..."

Wisdom 40

Verily the evil (or oppressive) actions will not be lost, even if they are few [that is they will be accounted for on the Day of Resurrection]. And every evil (or oppressive) action will be brought forth on the Day of Judgment, even if it just a little, or something small (or slight), and for this reason some of the *mufassireen* said about the meaning of (the verse):

"... If it be (anything) equal to the weight of a grain of mustard seed..."

(that) it means the evil actions, (even) if they are very small, Allaah (the Most High) will bring them forth.

Wisdom 41

Having *imaan* (faith) in the two names of Allaah, *Al-Lateef* (Subtle) and *Al-Khabeer* (Well-Aware), and these two names are mentioned together repeatedly in many verses of the Noble Quraan. The name *Al-Khabeer* returns in its meaning to having knowledge of hidden affairs, that is the knowledge of things which are extremely subtle and small, and in the utmost concealment, and thus what is more obvious is His knowledge of things which are apparent and clear.

As for the name *Al-Lateef*, then it has two meanings: The first is [the meaning which is similar to] *Al-Khabeer*. And the second meaning, is, 'The One who sends to His servants that which is good for them [or what they need and benefit from] by His subtleness and goodness in ways that they are not aware of'.

Wisdom 42

The status of the *salaah* (the prayers) and importance of its establishment [meaning regular performance on time] and [the importance] of raising the children protecting it [that is performing it regularly on time].

The *salaah* (prayers) is from the greatest of obligatory actions and the most illustrious of compulsory deeds that Allaah has made obligatory upon His servants, and it is the [main] column of the *deen* (religion) and the most confirmed *rukn* (pillar) after the two *shahaadas* (the declaration of faith), and it is the connection between the *'abd* (servant of Allaah) and his Lord, and it is the first thing he will be accounted for on the Day of Resurrection, and if it is correct then all his actions are correct, and if it is wrong (or void) then all his actions will be wrong (or void), and it the separating factor between a Muslim and a non-Muslim, establishing it is Imaan (having faith) and losing it [being careless or leaving it] is disbelief and transgression. Therefore, there is no *deen* (religion) for whoever has no *salaah*, and no place in Islaam for whoever left the *salaah* (prayer). And whoever protects it [that is establishes it] then it will be [for him as] light in his heart, on his face, in his grave, and during his resurrection, and it will be salvation on the Day of Judgment, and [he will be] resurrected amongst those whom Allaah has bestowed His favor, from the Prophets, *Siddiqeen* (the righteous truthful followers of the Prophets who were the first and foremost to believe in them), martyrs, and righteous, and they are the best of companions. And whoever does not protect [or establish] it [that is the salaah] then he will have no light, or evidence, or salvation on the Day of Judgment, and he will be resurrected with Fir'awn (Pharaoh), Hamaan, and Ubay ibn Khalaf, and we seek refuge in Allaah from that.

Wisdom 43

Teaching and training the children to enjoin the good and to forbid the evil from a small age. And in this is a great benefit for them and for others. This is because if the child is raised from childhood as a caller to good, then he benefits from this and others benefit from him.

As for the benefit that he gains, then his calling others [to good] will be a protection for him against them calling him to evil. And it has been said in the past, "If you do not call, you will be called" [that is if you do not call others to good, then they will call you to evil]. So if the child is a caller to good then that in itself will be protection for him against evil, because they [that is other people] know him to be a caller to good, so they will find no path to him [that is they will not be able to call him to evil, and they will give up on calling him to evil]. As for the benefit that comes to others (because of this), then maybe people will be guided through him, so their guidance will be on his scale of good deeds. The Prophet (peace and blessings of Allaah be upon him) said:

That one person should be guided through you, is better for you than the red camels.

[Note: Red camels are rare and were of extremely high value at that time.]

Wisdom 44

The advice to have patience, especially those calling to Allaah and those who order good and those who forbid evil should be patient, because their position is one that requires great patience.

...and bear with patience whatever befall you. Verily! These are some of the important commandments ordered by Allaah with no exemption.

Wisdom 45

No one rises to do actions upon these important commandments (which are ordered by Allaah with no exemption), except for those who have big *nufoos* [that is that they are strong over their nafs (selves) and have control over their nafs].

Wisdom 46

A warning against boasting and arrogance in the statement:

Verily, Allaah likes not each arrogant boaster...

Ibn Katheer (Allaah have mercy on him) said [in explaining this]: that is the arrogant is the one who is amazed by himself, [and] boaster: that is with others.

Wisdom 47

The call towards being in the middle and to be moderate:

"And be moderate (or show no insolence) in your walking, and lower your voice. Verily, the harshest of all voices is the voice (braying) of the ass"

Wisdom 48

Affirmation of Allaah's attribute of *mahhabah* (liking or loving).

Verily, Allaah likes not each arrogant boaster

Wisdom 49

The call of the *Shari'ah* to have the best of manners and its warning against the lowest of them [that is to have bad manners].

Wisdom 50

The importance of striking examples when teaching. So His statement:

... and lower your voice. Verily, the harshest of all voices is the voice (braying) of the ass is a an excellent and clear (or well spoken) example that raising the harsh and evil voice [is bad, because] if there was some benefit to it, then that animal, whose vileness and stupidity is known, would not have been chosen.

Conclusion

So these are some of the benefits which have been extracted from this blessed context. In any case, indeed these advices that Luqmaan advised his son will bring together the main parts of wisdom, and necessitates that which was not mentioned from it [meaning that what was said directly leads to what is understood indirectly if it was not mentioned], and every advice is brought together with that which it calls to in terms of doing actions, if it is an order, or to abandon, if it is a prohibition.

This points to what we mentioned in the definition of *hikmah* (wisdom), that it is the knowledge of rulings, the reasons for it, and its appropriate applications. So he [that is Luqmaan] ordered him [that is his son] with the foundation of the religion, which is *tawheed* (the worship of Allaah alone), and prohibited him from *shirk* and made clear to him the reason for leaving it.

He ordered him (his son) to be dutiful to the parents and explained to him the reason for that. He ordered him to be thankful to Him (Allaah) and to them (his parents) then [he] cautioned that being dutiful to them and carrying out their orders is to be so, as long as they do not order with disobedience [to Allaah], and that if it was so [that is if they did order him to disobey Allaah] then even still he is not to be disobedient [in a manner that is blameworthy], but rather he should be kind to them, even if he is not obeying them when they fight with him so that he does shirk. He also ordered him [to be mindful] of Allaah watching him, and scared him [by reminding him] of returning to Him (Allaah), and that He leaves nothing, no matter how small or big from good or evil deeds, except that He will bring it forth [on the Day of Judgment].

He forbade him from being arrogant, and ordered him to be humble. He forbade him from vanity, wildness, and rudeness, and ordered him to be calm in his movements and voice, and forbade him from the opposite of that.

He ordered him to command the good and forbid the evil, to establish the prayer and to have patience [two things] which with them makes every affair easy, as [Allaah] stated. So it is befitting that the one who advised with these advices to be specified with [the trait of] wisdom and famous for it. And for that reason it is from the blessing of Allaah and the rest of His servants that He relayed to them [that which is] from his wisdom, [and] what is a good example for them.

I ask Allaah (the Most High) by His beautiful names and lofty attributes to benefit us with what we learned, and to make what we learn to be a proof for us and not against us, and to provide us with beneficial knowledge and good actions. I ask Allaah (the Most High) to reward Luqmaan the Wise with the best of rewards and to forgive us and him and all Muslims - male and female, and all of the Mu'mineen (true believers) - male and female, those who are alive and those who have passed away, verily He is The Most Forgiving, The Most Merciful.

And Allaah knows best, and may Allaah send peace and blessings upon our Prophet.